Contents

Foreword

We hope you find the following contributions as inspiring as we did. Every piece of writing, poem, illustration and photograph has been especially commissioned for this book, and they all represent stories of survival, bravery and, ultimately, achievement.

All of these stories demonstrate courage and optimism: everyone who contributed has found a way to turn intensely difficult situations into positive outcomes. The strength, humour and sensitivity evident in these writings inspires us all, by showing how even the most traumatic experience can shape a person into becoming stronger than they could have imagined.

There are many different types of bullying described in this collection, taking place in a variety of settings and contexts. Obviously one of the more common venues where the bully can strike is at school, but what often goes unspoken about is the bullying that can occur during our adult lives - bullies are also at large in the community and in the workplace.

Often, the person who has suffered bullying can find themselves asking the question, "Why me?" as if there is a reason behind the bullying, a factor that somehow marks them out as deserving of such treatment. This collection of stories reveals that bullies will always find a target for their abuse, but there is *never* any justification for it.

In several of our stories, people who have been bullied are able to empathise with others in a similar situation and have offered their support to them in their hour of need. This indomitable spirit is the essence of our book and we feel it deserves to be celebrated. However, we are fully aware that not all victims of bullying are able to find a way out of their torment and there are several high profile cases each year where such people feel they are unable to continue with their lives. Our book is dedicated to these people and their families. We hope that this book can inspire anybody living with bullying not to give up hope and to use their experiences to find a positive outcome to their situation.

Royalties from the sale of this book will be donated to charities chosen by the writers.

Anthony's Story

When I was fifteen, I used to hang about the streets with people three or four years older than me, usually getting drunk or experimenting with drugs. I came from a large family so I suppose it was quite difficult for my parents to keep tabs on everything we did, and it was no surprise that they never knew I had stopped attending school. Half way through my last year, I was expelled for being drunk and left school with no qualifications. I found a job with my uncle in the building trade and worked every day for a year and a half, getting drunk at weekends. It was then that I met my future wife, who was five years older than me and had her own flat, which I moved into.

By the time I was eighteen, we had a daughter and we were all happy. I was doing well with my job, but I was drinking every night. Two years later, my son was born and we were living in a nice council house with the opportunity to buy. My drink problem became worse, but I refused to admit it to my friends, wife or family. Ten years passed as I swapped and changed from one job to another, not seeming to care about anything except the next drink and myself. Ultimately, my wife divorced me and I was out on the street with nowhere to go. My family didn't want to know me while I was still drinking and my so-called friends were nowhere to be seen.

It didn't really hit me that I was alone until I spent my first six or seven months on the streets of Manchester, begging and going to drop-in centres during the day, visiting the soup runs in the evening. I was about thirty at the time and felt that I could look after myself. How wrong I was. The number of times I've been put into hospital, robbed or beaten up, I still cannot count.

Around the age of thirty-five, I was given a flat by the Council, which I kept for four years - although not very well, as I would invite strangers in until it was impossible to get rid of them. Because of my good nature, I was bullied for money to buy drink, which I was totally dependent on to get through each day. This bullying went on endlessly, until I took such a beating that I had to spend three months in hospital.

Whilst there, as well as mending my bones,
I managed to detox from alcohol, but no sooner had I
been discharged and put into a hostel than I started
drinking again. There's a saying about 'burning your
bridges' - well the number of hostels, B and B's, dry
houses and wet houses that I've been evicted from,
I'd say most I couldn't rebuild.

I spent another three months on the streets until I had
lost all hope, all pride, self-esteem, worth, values,
everything. Not for the first time I tried to commit
suicide because I thought my life was so worthless.
Then I was taken in by Turning Point, who helped me
to abstain from alcohol and gave me hope, until I
started to believe in myself again. After being alcohol-
free for almost six months, I had new friends and the
confidence to do pretty much anything.

At forty-one years of age, I decided that I was going
to college to study to become a nurse. At first it was
nerve-racking, but I've met some lovely people at
college. The teachers are very understanding and will
help you regardless of how old you are or which
qualifications you don't have.

I finished my Access to Learning for Nursing course in June 2006. I also achieved certificates in Adult Numeracy and Adult Literacy at Level Two, which are equivalent to GCSE's. I have learned to use a computer and lots of relevant information that will help me in the future. With hard work, motivation and thankfulness for being given this opportunity despite my past life, I will gain two A levels which will enable me to enter university to study for a Diploma in Adult Nursing.

Everything seems to be working out for me now that I have got an aim in life - an ambition to do better for myself. Even my family are starting to accept me. My kids have got time for me now and I get to babysit my granddaughter whenever I'm needed. I'm so proud of my achievements from the age of forty that I don't even look back. If I can do it, then so can anyone. Life is what you make it and can be a happy and healthy one if you decide to fulfil your aim in life. There are lots of loving and caring people out there, so if you have read this, I hope it inspires you to look at life differently and see that it isn't all doom and gloom. Look after yourself and the rest will fall into place. Good luck!

Alison's Story

The bullying took place at school during Year 9 and Year 10. I was only 14 and the bullies were a year older than me. They called me names and threatened to beat me up after school. When I did tell a teacher, they found out and beat me up anyway because one of the girls was expelled.

I started drinking a lot and it messed my head up. I felt as though I was an outsider. As everyone else was with their friends laughing and joking, I was on my own - too scared to move from the room I was in. I sat in that room for five hours a day.

I felt on my own, as if no one wanted to know me. Although I did get support from teachers and other girls that were going through the same thing, it didn't help. I only felt safe when I was at home, but I knew I was missing out on my education. The teachers tried to keep me out of the way by putting me in the Learning Support Unit and reducing my time in school so I could go home earlier than the bullies and avoid them.

It knocked my confidence a lot. The only thing that took my mind off it was going to college to study hair-dressing. Luckily, one of the teachers found me some work experience in a hairdresser's, one day a week. When I finally left school, the hairdresser's salon gave me a full-time job, which helped me to meet and work with new people. I became more confident and assertive with people too.

My advice is to find something you are interested in to take your mind off what you are going through, and you may find that it becomes a job for life. I now have lots of friends to go out and socialise with and I don't drink like I did then. I am a lot happier now and I won't let anyone treat me the way they did.

After I left, they tried to make friends with me but I told them I didn't want to be friends with people like them.

Kathleen's Story

The first bullying humiliation I can remember was a long time ago. Yet somehow, it was to build and strengthen my character, to get me through a lifetime of bullying. It happened when I was ten years old. I had no books or writing materials and I was unable to read or write. One day, the girl next door gave me an old jotter and pencil and I felt over the moon with them, even though the jotter was very dirty and full of scribbles.

One day, my teacher was absent and we had to go to another teacher who was a friend of my usual teacher. She decided to make an exhibition of me. She pinned all the dirty pages to my back and made me walk round the whole school. She sent another girl with me to make sure I went into every class.

My main thought as I went from classroom to classroom was not to cry. I was not going to please her by giving in to tears. As I went along, all I could do was stare into space and pretend I was sleepwalking. In one class, there was a nice nun. She sent the other girl away and asked me my name. She asked who had done this to me and I told her. She took the papers off my back and led me by the hand, back to my class. I had a lot of trouble holding back the tears, but I managed it. She spoke to the teacher, but I did not hear what was said, as I am deaf. My teacher told me to go home. My legs were shaking like jelly. I wanted to run but couldn't. I was afraid to go home because I didn't want my mother to know what had happened. I stopped at the church on the way home and went into a little side chapel. I felt safe there and I let the tears flow, to ease my pain.

It's hard to know how it affected me as I was also being bullied at home by my brother-in-law. What I can say is the experience taught me to control my feelings, which helped me a lot as I was growing up. The best thing to do with a bully is to ignore them, because that is the one thing they hate. They love attention and hate law and order. If the situation gets out of hand, report them to whoever is in charge and look them straight in the eye.

What do I do?

My whole world is crashing down on me

Everyone that used to care... GAVE UP

Everyone I could turn to... RAN AWAY

Everyone I love... SIMPLY IGNORES

I don't know what to do

I just sit in my corner

The same corner I was in many times before

The corner that knows it all

The corner that has been flooded...

and dried up a million times

The corner that doesn't judge me

Those walls just join together to enclose me

A safe place where I can be me

I can let it all out

I can cry... and cry

Until no more tears will fall from my lonely eyes

Have you ever had a time

When you had no idea what to do?

I have those times all the time

I believe it's almost time... TO GIVE UP.

Curtis's Story

My experience of bullying came when I was eleven years old and in the third year of my primary school. The bullying carried on until I left the school at the end of the fourth year. The bullies were all in the same year as me and there were three of them. The main one was a boy named Sean.

I remember feeling very isolated because I didn't feel that I could speak to any of the teachers. I used to go into the cloakroom everyday and my packed lunch would be on the floor with parts of it missing. I think I felt more frustrated than scared at the time, because the three of them were always together and whenever I would challenge one of them, the others would become involved.

There was also an element of racism in there as well and this made me feel very upset because there weren't any other black or mixed race people in the school.

At the time, I just tried to avoid them, which wasn't always possible. I remember telling my form teacher on a number of occasions and he would say, "Just avoid them," and, "What are you doing to annoy them?" I never felt that anybody was taking it seriously in school and I soon realised that it wasn't going to change unless I found a way to challenge them. I eventually dealt with it by fighting back, both physically and verbally.

This experience has made me realise how much upset and stress bullies do cause. I realise that such experiences affect different people in different ways. It has made me more aware of the importance of challenging bullying behaviour. If anything, I would say that the experience has made me stronger, because it has made me realise that sometimes the bullies need help as much as the people who are being bullied.

It has also made me more aware of my own behaviour and views, because I have noticed that I am more likely to clash with people who tend to push people about or try to use some kind of intimidation.

I think one of the main barriers a person being bullied faces is a lack of support. If somebody is being bullied then they need to inform somebody who may be able to help. Also I think people being bullied sometimes feel as though there is something wrong with them. As a result, they seem to accept what is happening to them. If that person still feels the impact of being bullied, then accessing a youth centre or community centre could be useful, as some youth workers are skilled in using anti-bullying strategies.

A person's self-esteem is affected in a number of ways by bullying, so trying to increase a person's self-esteem can be helpful. Encourage a person to become part of a group or club, especially if there is a real 'team-player' kind of attitude. Athletics or martial arts can be good for some people and this, combined with advice or support, can have a dramatic effect.

Eve's Story

My teenage years were the worst of my life due to the severe depression I had suffered since I was twelve. However, my depression wasn't the only black cloud hanging over me at that time. As a fifteen year old girl I suppose I had the same insecurities as most girls of my age. I was popular though and had lots of friends. I also knew people I could trust and had a loving family. Now I am a mature, confident twenty-nine year old woman and it's difficult for me to try to make sense of what actually happened during those years. I do know that my experiences of bullying had an impact on my confidence for a long time - but not any more.

Although I was popular, I was also very shy and lacked confidence in certain situations, which probably made me an easy target for some people. I was no pushover though. Growing up around some of the toughest streets in Manchester, I knew how to defend myself when I needed to. I had to, we all had to.

It's very difficult for me to remember exactly how the bullying started. I think, because of all the other issues I was dealing with at the time, I had blocked a lot of it out of my head. I do remember one girl in particular targeted me. There had been rumours that an older lad fancied me. He pursued me and I rejected him. I then found out that he had been this girl's boyfriend, but that he had now ended their relationship. As far as I was concerned, their splitting up had nothing to do with me. She, however, had other ideas.

The girl didn't go to my school, although many of her friends did and I was always being told that she wanted to smash my face in so her ex wouldn't like me any more. She started hanging around outside the gates of my school where she would shout 'bitch', 'slag' or whatever else she felt like. This name-calling continued along with the threats. I tried to ignore it for as long as I could, until the anger and threats turned to violence.

One occasion stood out for me in particular. After a row with my parents, I decided to go and stay at my Gran's house one Friday night. At about 7 o'clock, I received a call from a friend who was babysitting in the area.

I decided to go and keep her company and I set off to join her. My friend was only a short distance down the road. I was looking forward to seeing her for a gossip.

As I turned into the street, I noticed that there were quite a few people who had gathered on the other side of the street, both girls and boys. I did feel a little intimidated and then I saw her, the girl who had made my life a misery. I made my way into the house where my friend was, thinking, "Shit, I've had it!" I noticed she was with her ex, which only made the situation worse.

The shouting started after about ten minutes. I could tell they were having a row and I remember her shouting, "Well if you want her, go and get her. And if you don't, I will!"

She began hammering on the door. I'd had enough and decided to confront her. The next thing I knew, I was being dragged out onto the street. A crowd of the same girls and lads I'd seen earlier had formed a circle around us. There was no way out. An argument began and then, bang! My left eye felt like it was going to explode. I fought back and was actually beginning to get a few good punches in, until it all changed. It was no longer the one-to-one situation it had started as, as I now had eight to ten other girls joining in as well. As you can imagine, I don't remember much else. My friend who was babysitting had called a couple of our mates to help out, but it was no use. There were simply too many of them.

They eventually backed off, but I was left battered, bruised and covered with blood. I was unrecognisable when I woke and had to go to my friend's house before any of my family saw me. I looked absolutely awful and was devastated when I looked in the mirror, but I know it could've been much worse.

Monday in school, everyone was talking about it. The headmaster even called the girl in and told her to back off - fat lot of good that did! Things did calm down after my older sister sorted the situation out, when she found out what had been going on.

As a twenty-nine year old woman looking back on events, I have a different perspective on the whole situation. At the time, I felt like it was my fault. I now know that it wasn't - it was all down to that girl's jealousy. It's as simple as that.

I suppose what I'm trying to say is that no matter how terrible things seem to be when you're going through an experience like that, you can come out the other side, much stronger and wiser. I have a beautiful son, great partner and job, a fabulous family and more friends than I could know what to do with. My life is happy and I will never, ever give the bullying another thought after writing this.

I don't care about any of the people involved in those events and I'm a great believer in fate and what goes around comes around. I still hate violence of any kind, especially girls fighting. I am a different person now from then, and if you are experiencing anything similar to me, you will be too one day.

The Gang

There's a gang in the playground and I'm so scared
They pulled my coat which was already teared
They laughed at me and thought it was funny
They called me names and took my money
They nicked my bag, ripped all my books
They said I was giving them dirty looks
It wasn't my fault, I wanted to cry
I couldn't tell the teacher, I'd have to lie
I picked myself up off the cold hard floor
I wanted to tell the teacher but they'd beat me more
I thought about it through the night
I hoped that it was going to be alright
So I went to school early on the next day
And I told the teacher what I had to say
After that I felt I'd won
And now I never get picked on.

Samir's Story

I am a Libyan teenager, living in England with my parents. They are studying at the University of Manchester and I have been studying English at City College for two years. I have many good friends here now but, when I first came, I had no one but my younger brother.

My family sent me to a school on Saturdays, where I learnt Arabic with other Arab children and young people. I went with my younger brother who is thirteen and my Libyan and Tunisian friends who are seventeen and sixteen. When I first started to go, it was just my brother and I. My father took us for the first few times, but then we had to catch the bus and make our own way there. We were worried that we might get lost.

One day, we were waiting to come home and the bus was late. We waited for a long time and I noticed some boys who were looking at us. I didn't tell my brother because I didn't want to worry him. The boys didn't do anything - they just stared at us, then the bus came and we went home.

A few weeks later, on a cold day in February, we were waiting and the same boys were there. This time, I was with another friend from school as well. I noticed that one of the boys had gone down a street and there were only four of them. They started to walk over to us, then they stopped. I knew they were going to do something. I looked for the bus, but it wasn't coming.

Then, from behind us, a stone hit my brother on the head, forcing him to cry out in pain. The boy who had gone away from the group had come round behind us and thrown it. Now the others came closer and started throwing sticks at us. They called out racist words and told us to go back home and warned us that if they saw us again, there would be trouble. I couldn't fight back because of my younger brother. He was hurt.

When we got back, we didn't tell our family. We were worried that they might stop us from going to the school and felt ashamed that we didn't fight back.

Next time we had to go, my brother said he was feeling ill. I had to go without him, but I felt better for this because I was going with a few more friends this time. The boys were there and they threw sticks and yelled at us again. They followed us to the school and waited outside. This happened many times and often my brother would pretend to be ill, so he couldn't go.

Once, a teacher noticed the boys shouting things outside the school and asked me what was going on. Although I was worried that people would think it was our fault and we would get into trouble, I told him the truth. I told him that the boys were attacking us and that it had been going on for many months. I told him this was the reason why some boys had not been attending and that we hadn't told anyone because we were scared of getting in trouble. I told him about the boys' violence and racist words. I told him how we had to put up with it every week, going to and coming home from the school.

The teacher called the police and we watched the boys run off when they came. The teacher took us back to Manchester and called our parents for a meeting. He explained the story to them and told them how the police had asked us all about the boys.

The school was moved to Hulme and we never had to see the boys again. We found out that a woman had seen the boys throwing sticks at us and had reported it. The boys had been warned not to go near us again. My father was very angry with the boys and, at first, with us for not telling him about it. He was pleased that we had told the teacher and that we were now safe.

I think we should have told the teacher and our parents sooner, as it would have stopped my brother being upset by what happened. Now I look back and see that we have all learned a lesson. My father is now more able to listen to us and we are sure he will believe us in the future.

Marie's Story

I started to get bullied the minute I stepped into secondary school. It started off with name-calling, but soon I was being physically pushed about. Once, I tried to stand up to the girl, but her friends said, "Hit her and we'll hit you!" I knew it was pointless, so I got up and ran out of the classroom and continued all the way home.

I started to pretend I was ill so I wouldn't have to go to school, but my mum got wise to it and made me go in. I threw myself down the steps at home, hoping to sprain my ankle so I could have a few days off. I ended up fracturing two bones in my spine and had to spend six weeks lying flat, with a board under my mattress, on my bed downstairs.

I remember once standing outside the dinner hall when one of the girls who regularly bullied me, pushed in front of me and said, "Bastards to the back of the line!" I was so humiliated.

I spent most of the next four years pegging off, even though I loved learning and school. I just hated the daily taunts about my looks, my hair and my clothes. The experience left me with little confidence, very low self-esteem and self-hatred.

I've seen the bullies since leaving school and I pity them. They haven't achieved any more than I have - maybe they let their bullying affect their future like I allowed it to affect my past. My life was made a misery not because of anything I did, but because I was skinny and made to have short hair; because my shoes or sweaters didn't have brand names; because I had freckles and didn't have a dad.

One positive thing to come from being bullied is that I don't care what people think of me. The only opinions that matter are those of true friends and loved ones. Nobody has a right to put someone down because they don't agree with their lifestyle or views, but definitely not because they don't like the way someone looks. If you don't like the way I look, then don't look at me! I'm not bothered.

I would never judge someone on their looks or their clothes, or on what they have or haven't got. I also feel the need to step in if I see it happening to someone else. I've worked most of my life in factories and warehouses, but recently went to college and achieved a Level Two qualification in Literacy. I'm only sorry I let the bullies ruin my education, but then maybe my life wouldn't be the same.

I'll be brave tomorrow

I'll be brave tomorrow and you know it
I'll wipe my eyes and I'll stand up tall
You won't hurt me any more you'll see
Your blows can knock me down but I won't fall

You're weaker than me really, it's clear
You're the one who's scared, more than me
I quiver and shake in your gaze, I know
But tomorrow I'll win, then I'll be free

That girl with the skinny legs and little pink eyes
She'll pay for this, and deserve it for being weak
I can't stand up to you Dad, you're too big
But tomorrow at school I'll show her and you
I'm not a freak.

Anne's Story

The bullying took place at work after my dad died. Although my boss had been supportive when my dad was rushed to hospital, this changed when I went back to work. I returned to work only a matter of days after the funeral, so I was feeling pretty raw, emotionally. It soon became clear that, in spite of all that had happened to me, my manager expected me to be back to 'normal' unrealistically quickly. Far from showing some understanding about my situation, my manager started piling more pressure on me to complete my duties. She emailed; she texted; she even phoned from home to make sure things were done, even though I'd been working nearly fifty hours a week.

I ended up being signed off work with stress and it was eighteen months after my father's death before I was able to return to work. Initially, it was very difficult to cope with. Many of my colleagues seemed distant towards me, mainly because they didn't want to be seen to take my side in the dispute.

Thankfully, outside work my close friends were very supportive. I was lucky that my husband and sons coped very well with the situation. I was also lucky to have a new boss when I started my phased return to work, who understood my situation and was very accommodating towards me. After building up my confidence steadily, I began to help the department towards a good set of results, which ultimately enabled me to get a promotion with another employer.

It has taken me a while to build up my confidence in my new job and I feel that I need more reassurance than I used to. On the plus side, I definitely value true friendship more than I used to and I think I now achieve a better work-life balance than before.

Here is my advice to people who may be experiencing similar problems to the ones I had in work:

- Hang on in there!
- Don't keep going too long on your own - seek help.
- Don't be afraid to seek medical help, if necessary, and don't be put off if you don't get a sympathetic hearing first time. Seek a second opinion if necessary.

- Similarly, get advice from Human Resources and if they are not sympathetic, ask to see someone else.
- Try to get access to a counsellor and treat them as an independent advisor who can help you to get things into perspective.
- Don't bottle things up, but try not to bore the same friend or colleague with your troubles as they may get tired of listening to you!
- Finally, good luck and be patient. You will come through it.

Jamal's Story

I'm seventeen years old and living in Manchester. I've just received a distinction from my course at college and, in a few years, I will be going to drama school to do a degree, which will hopefully lead to a career in performing arts. I feel really confident and positive about my life right now.

However, last year things were really different. I have been bullied since I was about fourteen. At first it was just name-calling and comments about me being dirty or about my appearance. Slowly, the remarks became nastier and comments were made about me being gay. Although I tried to ignore the bullies, the comments became more frequent until they were constant in every lesson. They were really nasty and I felt like the whole class had changed.

I went from being carefree and happy to being isolated and alone. Sadly, the teachers were no help at all. Because my confidence was so low, I started to feel so self-conscious that I stopped enjoying my favourite subjects, like drama. Even though I asked the teachers to stop the bullying, they didn't know what to do. I ended up just feeling embarrassed at having to discuss my sexuality with them, as I tried to explain why I was being bullied. I tried to get my mum to help, but she just told me to ignore it. The indifference of the teachers towards me and my situation meant that I had no one to help. I felt trapped. Imagine having to go somewhere every day that just causes you hurt and misery.

I decided the only way I could deal with this was to try to stay at home and get my mum to cover for me. I could not tell my brother as he would have used violence to put a stop to it and I didn't want that to happen, as I knew he would get in trouble. I spent a lot of time at home and the school only seemed interested in my absence, not the reasons behind it. I felt like they were part of the bullying too.

What do you do at that age? What do you do when you are fifteen and the teachers, who could put a stop to the bullying, don't do anything? How would you feel? I know now that many other people have been through this but at fifteen, you feel like you are the only one. It is lonely and very frightening. I am now at college trying to catch up with the two years of lost education caused by bullying. Now, I feel like I can cope with my sexuality and who I am and how I act. I have not changed my personality and I think I have come through it with a greater understanding of myself and others. I think the bullies were actually scared of themselves and of me.

I would advise anyone going through the kind of homophobic bullying that I suffered, to think about what it is that causes it. It is not you or something that you do; it is something in the bully. It is a fear of themselves or what they might be and they are trying to deflect their own problems onto others.

What you can do is demand that teachers do something about it. Contact your local Gay and Lesbian support group or School's Out, who support gay and lesbian young people across the country. Don't let bullies control you or what you do. Don't let these frightened people ruin your life or intimidate you. Leave them behind.

Lisa's Story

I was the only kid from my primary school to go to the Grammar School. All my friends carried on their education at the local Catholic High School, which did not have the same reputation for success. My parents felt that the grammar school was the best way for me to receive a classic English education because I did well in my exams. As an only child, I was excited, as I'd been reading *Mallory Towers* and *The Twins of St. Clare's* books, so I imagined a jolly school where I could be a bit of a tomboy and would be popular with everyone. This was during the late 1980's and by then, the school was not as posh as people thought it was. The first few weeks were fine and people were very friendly. All the first years stuck together to support each other and I got on fine in lessons and in the playground too.

Everything changed one day in October. A group of girls I had been friendly with decided that I was different. I read books and liked weird music, like the

Beatles, Velvet Underground, David Bowie and Punk. This was too much for my fellow eleven year olds. It became obvious that I was bright and that the teachers were impressed with me. I scored 100 per cent in a maths exam and my form tutor announced this 'astounding result' to the class. Also, as I was Catholic and my peers were Church of England, R.E. lessons became embarrassing as I was always being asked for the 'Catholic perspective'. My parents were not well off, whereas the other students had wealthy families who came from the villages outside the town. All these differences marked me out - I was about to experience bullying.

On that day in October, I had double physics first thing. The physics lab had large, wooden benches that seated six to a bench. I arrived in good time and took my normal place at the bench. I didn't realise for about five minutes what was happening but slowly, a sick, uneasy fear started to grow in me. For the first time in my life, I felt powerless and humiliated. The rest of the class had crowded around all the other benches, leaving me alone on my bench. The entire class had created an exclusion zone around me.

I was officially weird and deserved isolation. The class started singing, "She loves you, yeah, yeah, yeah!" at the top of their voices. I remember thinking that they weren't even singing the right Beatles stuff; I liked their later stuff. The teacher arrived and, as he was probably the most useless teacher in the school, he didn't have a clue what to do and was unable to control the uproar. I ended up leaving the class, saving my tears until I was in the corridor. I cried all the way to the school secretary's office and sat out the rest of the morning until I went home at lunchtime.

My parents advised me to, "Get on with it - ignore them; they'll soon move onto someone else, they're only jealous." I accepted this and went back to school the next day, less carefree and more introverted. During the next few weeks, many nasty remarks were thrown my way. I learnt to control every emotion and carried on doing well - achieving and attending. Because my results were good, the teachers had no cause for concern.

During my second year, the girls started a new campaign. They thought I was a dog, so they started barking at me every time they saw me. Between the lessons, in the corridors, in the toilets, "Woof, woof!" wherever I went. The other year groups soon picked this up and, because I never reacted, I suppose many students didn't realise the damage they were doing to my self-esteem.

I'm not sure how long this went on for. Every day there were new torments, new insults. By the end of the second year, I had accepted my fate as one of the 'weird' ones and joined the 'stiffs'. My new friends all felt socially excluded in one way or another. Two of us were too clever and 'swotty'; two were in the Christian Union and good at Latin; three of the girls had physical disabilities; another was in the school orchestra. We gathered together to protect ourselves. This way, there was always someone to sit next to; someone to be with while you ignored the tricks and teasing from the 'normal' kids.

Being bullied as a child is a life-changing experience and should be confronted and dealt with by the adults in that child's life. Children need to learn how to cope with the big, bad world, not cut themselves off from it.

They need to believe that teachers and parents can protect them, or at least acknowledge when bullying is taking place. In my case, because I was attending, achieving and taking part in clubs and activities, no one looked beneath the surface to explore my emotional needs.

I feel that because of this treatment, my twenties were quite difficult for me and I struggled to make happy relationships with people. It was as if I was comfortable being bullied - it made sense to me and I tended to choose relationships that reflected this.

Now I feel more confident, I can believe people when they say nice things about me. I believe that I deserve success, a happy relationship and all the good things in life. I also feel very strongly about people being unfairly treated and have developed a career based on helping the most marginalised in our society. Over the last ten years I have worked with unemployed teenagers, homeless young people, drug misusers, people experiencing mental distress, excluded pupils, children in the criminal justice system and refugees and asylum seekers. I have had enormous satisfaction empowering vulnerable young people to achieve their potential.

My experience did have one nice moment: in the sixthform, many of my peers discovered retro music. The Doors, Jimi Hendrix and Punk suddenly became the soundtrack to the common room. A boy turned to me and said, "You've always been into this music, haven't you?" I wanted to explode with outrage but, instead, I accepted his compliment with good grace. What had marked me out as weird when I was eleven was now interesting to my peers; weird was cool and, suddenly, so was I.

Rebecca's Story

When I was twenty-three, I met my then partner. He was charming, good-looking and had a great job. He was also extremely attentive and generous. I fell for him and we stayed together for six years, living together for five and a half of them.

The bullying and controlling started when we moved in together. It started with comments about what I was wearing and where I was going. He said he did this because he loved me so much and I believed him. He also started to be rude to my friends and family and made it difficult for them to visit the house. He said they were all using me and that he was protecting me. He was never rude to my parents because he knew that would be going too far, and that I would listen to them and not him.

I started to feel isolated and became more dependent on him. He convinced me people were trying to split us up and that no one else would ever want me. Every time I was supposed to go out with friends, he would cause so much trouble, that I gave up in the end. The bullying involved telling me I dressed like a 'slag' and putting me down verbally for everything, from my cooking to the way I cleaned the house. He told me that nobody liked me and that I couldn't make friends. He would also bully my friends by being aggressive and rude to them. He even bullied his own friends by putting them down and saying nasty things about them. He would deliberately put them down in front of other people to embarrass them. He expected to be driven everywhere and constantly criticised me.

I became more and more isolated from everyone because I believed what he was telling me. When he went too far, he would charm me with flowers and take me out for meals until I fell for it all over again. I became emotionally dependent on him because I was so isolated. Prior to meeting him, I was a confident, strong person; I had good friends and a job I really liked.

I coped with it by letting him take charge of everything, from what we ate to where we went on holiday. I didn't get to see *Coronation Street* for five years because he wouldn't let me watch what I wanted on the television. I began to feel so isolated. I believed that nobody liked me and that nobody could ever love me as much as he did. I felt unable to stand up to him in an argument because he was so aggressive. So in the end, I just went along with whatever he wanted. I began to drink more to cope with the situation and I pretended to stay in work because I dreaded going home. I began to feel anxious all the time and lost my confidence around other people. I was frightened that he would leave me on my own.

Things started to change when a new person began working with me. She wasn't easily intimidated and wasn't scared of him. She came to visit me and didn't let him bully her. My friends began to rally round and I realised that they weren't using me and that they did like me.

It took a long time for me to leave him and it definitely wasn't easy but, with the support of family and friends, things began to change. A friend started to go out with his mother and she treated him in a similar way to how her son treated me. Seeing this behaviour from the outside made me realise how wrong it was to put up with it. My friends had never given up on me and they supported me as I began to get my confidence back and started having fun and feeling happy.

It took four months for him to leave after I asked him to. During this time, he brought other women back to the house. I didn't care about the other women, as I realised I had turned a corner. When he finally left, I felt relieved and knew that I had done the right thing.

I met my husband two years later and during those two years, I had a ball. I am now happily married to a kind, handsome, caring man who tells me I am beautiful. I have a gorgeous daughter, great friends and I run my own thriving business. What I have now is real love - something I never had with him.

You can survive what happened to me. Don't give up on yourself, you are worth more. There are a lot of people out there who will help you to leave people like my ex. I am living proof of it.

Contributors to this book

The Write About... Group

From left to right: Andrew Ewen, Skills for Life and English Lecturer, Stockport College; Vicky Duckworth, Senior Lecturer in Post Compulsory Education & Training, Edge Hill University; Andy Armstrong, Learning Support Co-ordinator, City College Manchester; Bernie Horan-Healiss, Skills for Life & Maths Lecturer, Stockport College; Liza Monaghan, Principal Policy Officer Children's Services, Manchester City Council; Catherine White, Director, Gatehouse Media; Eve Bell, Complementary Health Lecturer, Stockport College.

Write About...

The Write About... Group was founded in 2006 by Bernie Horan-Healiss and Catherine White, who brought together a group of lecturers, tutors, researchers and mentors working in a variety of college, community and outreach education settings, sharing the common aim of helping people to work through their issues by writing about them.

Don't just think about it, write about it!

Our first Write About... project focused on the issue of bullying, oft-cited as a barrier to learning. The experiences of those who have been bullied can have a profound impact on their lives. By encouraging people to write about their experiences, they may be able to come to terms with them and, in doing so, provide hope and inspiration to others in similar situations.

A series of writing workshops, one-to-one writing support sessions and independent work has produced this varied collection of writings, illustrations and photographs, drawn from experiences of bullying in school, in the workplace, in the community and at home.

We wish to give special thanks for their support to Jane Wedderburn, Peter Roberts, Niina Marttilla, Student Services and all the staff at Stockport College; Robert Smedley, Dean of the Faculty of Education, Edge Hill University; Ray Dwerryhouse, Head of Department, Edge Hill University; and to all the writers, artists and photographers who have contributed to this book.

For more information about the Write About... Group and future projects, please email: writeabout@gatehousebooks.com.

Support organisations

Kidscape is a charity established specifically to prevent bullying and child sexual abuse. Helpline: 08451 205 204 for parents, guardians or relatives of bullied children. Website: www.kidscape.org.uk

BullyingUK is an online resource providing information on a variety of bullying issues. Website: www.bullying.co.uk

ChildLine offers a children's helpline. Telephone 0800 1111 to talk about any problem with a counsellor. ChildLine also provides online resources to help combat bullying. Website: www.childline.org.uk

Anti-Bullying Network is a school-related anti-bullying website for young people and their families. Website: www.antibullying.net

School's Out is working towards equality in education for lesbian, gay, bisexual and trans people. Website: www.schools-out.org.uk

Mind is the leading mental health charity in England and Wales. Website: www.mind.org.uk

The Workplace Bullying Institute (USA) is a non-profit organisation which campaigns against workplace bullying. Website: www.bullyinginstitute.org

Bullying Canada is a youth anti-bullying website: www.BullyingCanada.Ca

Kids Help Line Australia offers a free, confidential and anonymous, 24-hour telephone and online counselling service specifically for young people aged between 5 and 25. Telephone 1800 55 1800. Website: www.kidshelp.com.au

The listing of an organisation does not represent an endorsement by the Write About... Group or the publisher, nor do we accept responsibility for the availability or content of the websites referred to. The organisations listed have not endorsed this book.

Gatehouse Books®

Gatehouse Books are written by and for young people and adults who are developing their basic reading and writing skills. Their ideas and experiences make fascinating material for any reader, but are particularly relevant for adults working on their own reading and writing skills. The writing often strikes a chord with the reader - a shared experience of struggling against many odds.

The format of a Gatehouse Adult Beginner Reader is clear and uncluttered. The language is familiar and the text is often line-broken, so that each line ends at a natural pause.

Gatehouse Books are widely used within Adult Basic Education throughout the English speaking world. They are also a valuable resource within the prison education and probation services, social services and secondary schools.

Available from

Gatehouse Media Limited
PO Box 965
Warrington
WA4 9DE
England

Tel: 01925 267778
E-mail: info@gatehousebooks.com
Website: www.gatehousebooks.com

and from

avantibooks limited
The iO Centre
Unit 9 Whittle Way
Arlington Business Park
Stevenage
SG1 2BD